KNIGHTS & ARMOUR

This edition:
© **Book Life 2015**
Book Life
King's Lynn
Norfolk PE30 4LS

First edition
2006 © Aladdin Books Ltd.
PO Box 53987
London SW15 2SF

ISBN 978-1-910512-06-7

Cover Design by:
Matt Rumbelow

Cover Photo by:
Nejron Photo/shutterstock.com

Title Page Photo by:
Mel Nik/shutterstock.com

Illustrators:
Susanna Addario,
Alessandro Baldanzi,
Francesca D'Ottavi,
Paola Ravaglia,
Roberto Simone –
McRae Books, Florence, Italy

BookLife

KNIGHTS & ARMOUR

HEROIC **H** HISTORY

JIM PIPE

BookLife

CONTENTS

INTRODUCTION

Knights were armoured soldiers who fought on horses. In the movies, they are often heroes, brave in battle yet gentle and kind at court. Some real knights were like this, but it can be hard to tell the true stories from legends such as King Arthur.

Real knights did wear shining armour and rode on beautiful horses. Some were famous for their bravery and their fighting skills. Others, however, were bloodthirsty rogues. Despite their armour, they could be cut down by arrows and cannon.

Knights lived in Europe over 500 years ago. This book also looks at mounted soldiers from other times and places, from Japanese knights called samurai to Mongol archers and Russian cossacks. Read on – and discover how fighting men have made horses their best friend throughout the ages.

PART 1: ANCIENT TIMES – WAR HORSES

To Stone Age humans, horses were a tasty meal rather than a way to get around. By about 3000 BC, tribes in Central Asia used horses to work the land.

It was another thousand years before people learned how to ride. Horses were soon being bred for different jobs. Large, heavy horses carried armoured warriors into battle. Light horses raced in the ancient Olympic games.

Bolas

Horse Hunters ▼

Cave paintings from France show that horses were a favourite food for Stone Age hunters 15,000 years ago. Hunters used spears and bolas, pieces of rope with a heavy weight at the end to trip horses' legs up.

Horse Manual

We know horses were first used to pull chariots in Syria around 1700 BC. A Mitanni horseman wrote on clay tablets how to train chariot horses - the very first book on horses!

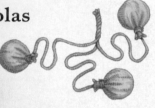

◀ Mongolian Wild Horse

The last remaining species of wild horse is similar to those hunted in the Stone Age.

A Sign of Wealth ▶

To the Ancient Greeks, the horse was a majestic animal ridden by heroes and gods. Horses were a sign of wealth as it was so expensive to keep them. Wealthy Greek citizens were called *hippes*, or knights.

◀ The First Knights

Early warriors rode bareback – it was easy to fall off! The invention of the stirrup around 400 AD allowed mounted knights to fight in armour. For 1,000 years they ruled the battlefield. Even today, cavalry are a symbol of power.

◀ Wild Stallions Fighting

The first riders to mount wild horses must have been very brave.

Myth and Legend ▶

Heroic knights appear in many myths and legends, from Greek centaurs to stories of King Arthur. These stories inspired later writers. In Lord Alfred Tennyson's poem *The Lady of Shalott* (1842), a cursed woman falls in love with a knight, Sir Lancelot.

CHARIOTS

Chariots were used as platforms to shoot or fight from. From around 1500 BC, they were used in huge numbers – 6,000 chariots fought at the Battle of Kadesh in 1298 BC. It took three years to train a team of horses and riders (who practised on a rocking stool!) At first, horsemen were used just for scouting, but by 600 BC, they began to replace chariots.

Stirrup

▲ **Stirrups**
The stirrup reached Europe around 800 AD. Saddles had arrived some 300 years earlier. They allowed an armoured knight to fight from a horse.

Sumerian chariot

Egyptian chariot

▲ **Clash of the Chariots**
The light chariots of Pharaoh Ramesses II carried archers. At the Battle of Kadesh, his forces were ambushed by large, heavily-armed Hittite chariots that smashed through the Egyptian battle lines.

◄ **Sunk!**
In the Bible, God's parting of the Red Sea saves Moses and the fleeing Israelites and drowns the Egyptian chariots sent to kill them.

Roman Cavalry ▶

They looked fierce, but without stirrups, Roman cavalry could barely swing a sword without falling off their horse. They were mostly used for chasing fleeing enemies.

Bareback Riders

The Roman cavalry was no match for the Numidians who fought for Hannibal. Riding bareback, they controlled their horses using their legs and voice rather than their hands.

▼ At the Races

The ancient Romans loved chariot racing. Chariots often crashed into each other, killing horses and riders. Many drivers were teenagers, as they were tall but light.

▲ Ass Attack

Around 2500 BC, the Sumerians were among the first to build chariots. The chariots were pulled by wild asses and had solid wheels. They carried spear throwers.

Alexander the Great ▶

loved his horse Bucephalus so much he named a city after it!

9

BEASTS OF WAR

Though his own father drowned while riding an elephant, it didn't stop Carthaginian general Hannibal from using these mighty creatures in a sneaky attack on the Romans.

In 218 BC, Hannibal led an army of 30,000 men and 37 elephants over the Alps. Despite battles with Celtic tribes and passes blocked by snow, he crossed the mountains in 15 days.

▼ Pegasus and Centaurs

Horses appear in many Greek myths. A winged horse, Pegasus, helped the hero Bellerophon defeat Chimaera, a monstrous mix of a lion, snake and goat.

When Greek merchants first saw horsemen near the Black Sea, they brought back stories of centaurs, beasts that were half-horse, half-man!

Pegasus

Hidden in a Horse ▼

In Homer's story, *The Odyssey*, Greek soldiers hid inside a wooden horse. When the Trojans pulled the horse inside their city, the Greeks climbed out and opened the gates to their army. Soon Troy was captured.

Trojan Horse

A unicorn looks like a white ▶ horse with a horn on its forehead. It appears in myths from China, India and Europe.

◀ **Living Tanks**
At first, the Roman soldiers and horses were terrified by the size, smell and loud trumpeting noise of Hannibal's elephants. In time, the Romans used fire to make the elephants panic, making them trample their own troops.

Camel warrior

Stinky Tactics ▶
At the Battle of Thymbra in 546 BC, the horses ridden by King Croesus' men were spooked by the awful smell of the camels in Persian King Cyrus' army.

In the 8th century AD, Arab armies also found that the smell of camels scared horses that were not used to them.

THE FIRST KNIGHTS

In 378 AD, the Goths defeated the Romans at Adrianople. They and the Avars showed how a cavalry charge by mounted troops could destroy soldiers on foot.

A hundred years later, invaders from Asia, such as the Huns, showed another way to fight. They rode on small, fast ponies and used short bows to shoot from horseback.

Goth

▼ Victory – But Only Just

Mounted troops didn't always win battles easily. When William the Conqueror invaded England in 1066, he met the Saxons at the Battle of Hastings. At first, his Norman knights struggled against the Saxon foot soldiers, who fought side-by-side using great two-handed axes.

When the Normans pretended to run away, however, the Saxons ran after them and were easily killed. Using this tactic again and again, the Normans won the battle.

The Battle of Hastings

In the Eye? ▶
In the Bayeux Tapestry, the Saxon king, Harold, is shown with an arrow in his eye. He was probably wounded by the arrow, then cut down by Norman knights.

▼ Hun warriors could shoot an arrow while riding at full speed.

◄ Charlemagne
Charlemagne (742-814 AD), king of the Franks, used his heavy cavalry to win a series of battles against Arabs, Saxons, Avars and Vikings. Horses, armour and weapons were very expensive, so Charlemagne rewarded knights who fought for him with land – known as the "feudal system".

Hun

◄ The Avars fought with swords, spears and bows and arrows.

Arab horseman

Knights in Armour
In October 732, the Franks under king Charles Martel defeated the Arabs at Poitiers in France. Though the Franks won fighting on foot, Martel was impressed by the Arab cavalry. He created the first knights in Europe – armoured soldiers who, thanks to stirrups, could fight on horseback.

Charles Martel

PART 2: THE AGE OF THE KNIGHT – BATTLEWINNERS

Knights were a medieval king's most important warriors in battle. They were also rich men, as paying for horses and armour was very expensive. Nobles had their sons trained as knights. It took many years.

At six or seven, boys became pages and worked for other nobles. They learned how to ride and fight and became squires, helping older knights to prepare for battle. When their training was over, squires became knights by taking an oath of loyalty.

King John

Château- ▶ Gaillard was not captured by mounted knights but by soldiers climbing into the castle, using a toilet window!

Capturing Castles

Big battles between knights were spectacular – but not always that decisive. Capturing enemy castles was more important. After a French army took Château-Gaillard from the English King John in 1204, it conquered huge areas of land nearby.

Knight in 1200

Excalibur

◄ King Arthur

King Arthur is a legendary knight who may have fought against the Saxon invaders of Britain in the 500s. However, he became a romantic hero thanks to the stories of the monk Geoffrey of Monmouth, who wrote in the 12th century.

Geoffrey's Arthur lives in his castle at Camelot and fights with Excalibur, a magical sword. French writers added other elements to the story, such as Sir Lancelot, the Knights of the Round Table and the Holy Grail.

Knights fought ▼ with lances, swords and axes.

Knight in 1500

▲ What a Mess!
A battle between knights was total chaos! First, they charged each other. Some were knocked off their horses. Those who weren't hurt carried on fighting on foot with swords.

ARMS AND ARMOUR

Sword

A knight's main weapons were his lance and sword. A lance was a wooden spear with a steel tip, used to knock an enemy off his horse. At first, swords had a broad, flat blade. As knights wore more armour, swords became thinner, so they could stab into the gaps.

Early knights wore chain-mail over a padded garment and carried large shields. By the 1400s, their whole bodies were covered in plates of steel.

Halberd
An axe on top of a pole.

1100

1225

Weighed Down? ▶

It was hard, hot work fighting in a suit of armour weighing 25 kg. But armour was light enough for a knight to get up quickly if he fell off his horse.

Knights also used mail, leather and steel plates to protect their horses.

Horse Armour

1350

◀ Head Gear

In the 1100s, helmets had a nose bar. By the 1400s, they covered the whole head.

1450

Dressing for Battle ▶

1500

Squires helped a knight dress for battle. Plates were fixed to an undershirt with laces.

◄ Chain-mail
In the 1100s, knights wore a tunic made up of metal rings that stretched down to their knees. They also wore a mail hood to protect their neck.

Coats of Arms ►
To show who they were, early knights had badges painted onto their tunics, which they wore over their armour. These family badges became known as their "coat of arms", which were joined together when two families married:

1 A lord's son and an important lady have their own coats of arms.

2 The coats are combined (called impaling).

3 When the lady's father dies, the coat of arms changes again.

4 When the lady's husband dies, her son's coat of arms is divided into four quarters.

A Coat of Arms

Heraldry ►
The system of family badges is known as heraldry.

1

2

3

4

THE CRUSADES

In 1095, Pope Urban II called for a holy war to free Jerusalem from the Muslim Turks. Thousands of knights made their way to the Holy Land. By 1099, these Crusaders had taken Jerusalem and set up four Christian "kingdoms". To defend the Holy Land, they built castles and created special teams of knights. But in 1187, Jerusalem was recaptured.

Though there were seven other crusades, all failed. When Muslims captured the city of Acre in 1291, the Crusaders lost the Holy Land forever.

A Bloody Victory ▶
At Antioch, a priest, Peter Barthelemy, claimed he had found the spear that pierced Christ's side.

This holy relic, real or fake, inspired the crusading knights to capture Jerusalem a few weeks later.

Once inside, they killed so many people that "men rode in blood up to their knees".

◀ Saladin
The Saracen general Salah ed-din, or "Saladin", retook Jerusalem in 1187 after destroying the Christian army at the Battle of Hattin. Unlike the bloodthirsty Crusaders, he allowed the inhabitants of Jerusalem to leave in peace.

Red Cross ▶
Most of the Crusaders returned home. They wore a red cross on their tunic as a sign of victory.

▲ Truce
The Third Crusade, led by English king Richard the Lionheart, defeated Saladin in battle, but failed to win back Jerusalem. In 1192, the two warriors agreed a truce allowing Christian pilgrims to visit holy sites in Jerusalem.

◀ The Siege of Jerusalem

◀ El Cid (The Lord)
In the 1100s, Rodrigo de Vivar, or "El Cid", became a Christian hero in Spain (his life was made into a movie). In fact, when it suited him, he also fought for Muslim rulers!

THE MONGOL HORDES

In the 1200s, the Mongol army swept across Asia, conquering a vast empire that stretched from China to the Black Sea.

Trained from youth to be expert riders and archers, the Mongols relied on speed rather than heavy armour. Unlike European knights, they were very organised. First they attacked with lances and swords, then a second wave threw spears and shot arrows.

Khan The Conqueror

The Mongol tribes were united by Genghis Khan, whose name means "greatest of rulers". After conquering North China, his hard-riding horde swept through Turkestan, Persia, India and Russia. The Mongols showed no mercy – they wiped out whole cities, even the cats and dogs!

Milking a horse

◀ **Mongol soldiers** could travel ten days while eating only their horses' milk and blood. If a horse got sick, each man had a spare.

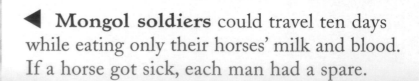

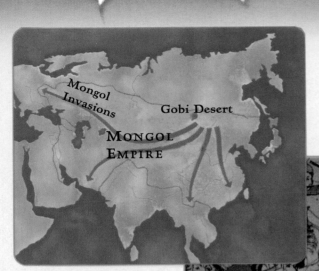

Mongol Invasions
Gobi Desert
MONGOL EMPIRE

Genghis Khan's Empire

▼ **Mongols 9 – Knights 0**
The Mongols met Christian knights in battle at Liegnitz, Hungary, in 1241. They filled nine sacks with the ears of the dead knights!

◄ **Whistling Messages**
The Mongols used different arrows for piercing armour or slicing flesh. Whistling arrows told their troops which way to turn.

Invasion on Ice ►
Batu, a grandson of Genghis, invaded Europe in 1237-1240. Using the frozen rivers as roads, his Mongols crossed the Volga river, burned down Moscow then captured Kiev.

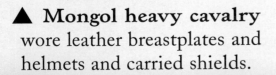

▲ **Mongol heavy cavalry** wore leather breastplates and helmets and carried shields.

THE SAMURAI

The knights in Japan were called samurai. At first they guarded the emperor's palace and were famous for their riding and archery skills. After 1185, when Minamoto Yoritomo became *shogun* (military ruler), the samurai were masters of Japan.

They formed large armies and fought with razor-sharp samurai swords. Like European knights, they also followed a code of honour, called *bushido*.

▼ Samurai Armour
At first, armour was made from small metal or leather scales. In the 1500s, samurai starting wearing solid metal plates to protect them from firearms.

▲ Helmets
were decorated with feathers, antlers and even buffalo horns!

Warrior's Way
Bushido, "The Way of the Warrior", expected samurai to be loyal, honourable, polite, expert at martial arts and willing to die at any time.

The Samurai Coat of Arms ▶

When samurai went into battle, the air was filled with *sashimono*, the small flags that every warrior wore on his back. These showed which warlord he was fighting for. When a defeated samurai had his head cut off, it was wrapped in this flag.

▼ **Sashimono**, the flags worn by samurai.

Cut to Ribbons

Samurai were brave and tough - one warrior kept fighting after receiving 13 sword slashes. At Uji in 1184, two samurai raced each other to be the first into battle.

▼ **Kabuki** plays often retold legends about heroic samurai.

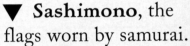

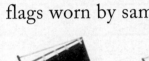

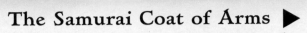

▲ The fearless **Tomoe Gozen** was a famous female samurai warrior.

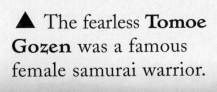

PIKES AND LONGBOWS

Most foot soldiers didn't stand a chance against knights. They had little armour or training, and they were often trampled by their own side.

However, armed with a longbow, English foot soldiers defeated a much larger army of French knights at Crécy, France, in 1346. After shooting down their horses, they leapt on the fallen knights and stabbed them.

▼ Form a Hedghog!

In the 1400s, Swiss soldiers borrowed an ancient Greek idea. They fought in a tight bunch with pikes: 6m long poles with a metal spike at the end. When surrounded, the pikemen formed a "hedgehog", with pikes on all sides. At the Battle of Morat, in 1476, they destroyed a powerful army of knights.

Pikemen

▲ At **Agincourt** in 1415, 6,000 English soldiers again defeated an army of 20,000 French knights by using longbows.

They were helped by thick mud, which bogged down the French horses when they charged.

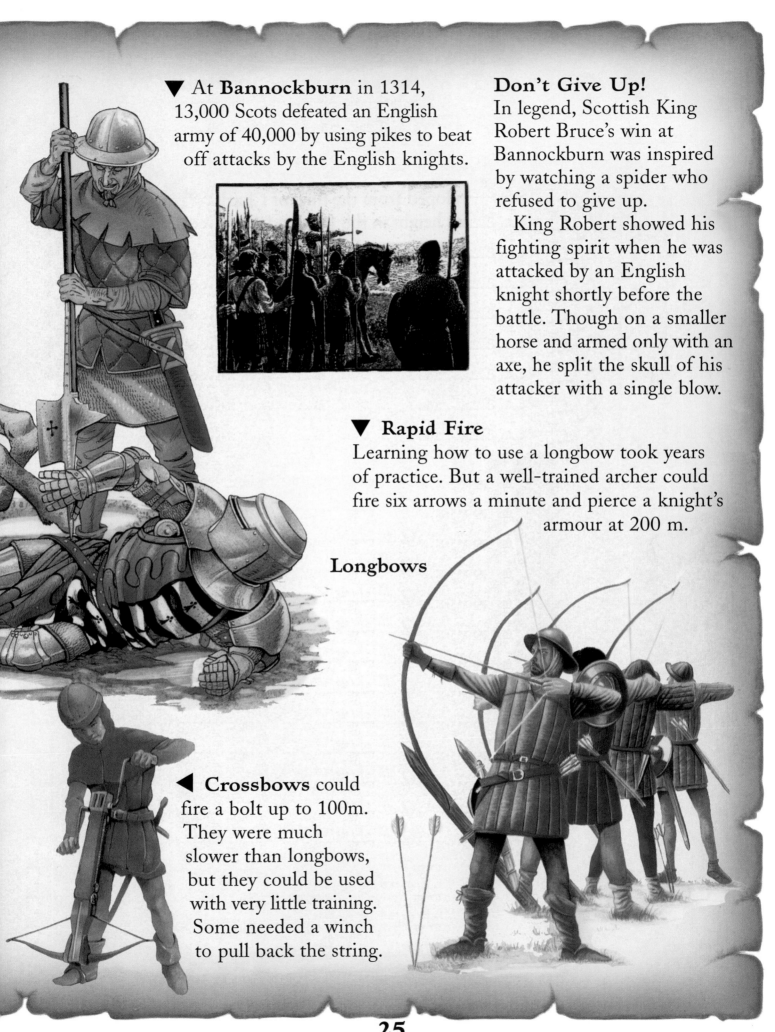

▼ At **Bannockburn** in 1314, 13,000 Scots defeated an English army of 40,000 by using pikes to beat off attacks by the English knights.

Don't Give Up!

In legend, Scottish King Robert Bruce's win at Bannockburn was inspired by watching a spider who refused to give up.

King Robert showed his fighting spirit when he was attacked by an English knight shortly before the battle. Though on a smaller horse and armed only with an axe, he split the skull of his attacker with a single blow.

▼ Rapid Fire

Learning how to use a longbow took years of practice. But a well-trained archer could fire six arrows a minute and pierce a knight's armour at 200 m.

Longbows

◄ **Crossbows** could fire a bolt up to 100m. They were much slower than longbows, but they could be used with very little training. Some needed a winch to pull back the string.

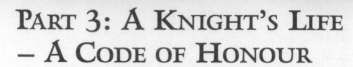

Part 3: A Knight's Life – A Code of Honour

At first, knights were just mounted soldiers, but a code of rules grew up that expected them to be loyal to their king. During the Crusades, knights were also inspired by Christian ideas, which taught them to be gentle, polite and humble, and poetry, which talked about love and honour. These ideals, called "chivalry", tried to set a good example. Sadly, they didn't stop knights from being cruel and brutal.

▼ Becoming a Knight

There were strict rules about how a knight should fight, dress, eat or hunt. There were also important rituals, such as putting on a sword when first becoming a knight.

The Dragonslayer ▲
St. George was an early Christian saint. By the Middle Ages, he had become a romantic hero, famous for rescuing a fair maiden from a dragon.

▼ Chivalry expected knights to honour and protect women.

Winning your spurs was a sign of being a knight – but Edward III's son, the Black Prince, won his at the Battle of Crécy while fighting on foot!

Spurs

The Green Knight ▶
In medieval legend, Sir Gawain beheads a giant green knight, who calmly puts his head back on and tells Gawain it's his turn next! A year later, when Gawain offers his head, the green knight spares him, saying he was sent to test his chivalry.

◀ A Medieval Quest
In legend, the Holy Grail is the cup that Jesus drank from during the Last Supper. It was said to have been brought to Britain but was later lost.

King Arthur's knights go on a quest to find it, but only Sir Galahad sees the grail.

The Holy Grail has also appeared in movies ▼ such as *Monty Python and the Holy Grail* and *Indiana Jones and the Last Crusade*. Other films, such as *The Court Jester* and *Jabberwocky*, make fun of chivalry.

THE FEUDAL SYSTEM

The world that a knight lived in was based on the "feudal system". Every country was ruled by a king or duke. The king handed out power and land to his lords, who swore an oath to support him.

Each lord then gave land to his knights, who promised to train soldiers for him. At the bottom, poor people called serfs worked the land, in return for their lord's protection.

◀ Men for Money

In the 1500s, the feudal system broke down: soldiers now wanted money not land. To go to war, kings had to borrow money from bankers.

The paid soldiers, called "mercenaries", were not loyal to one lord - they fought for anyone who could pay them.

Chess, with its kings, queens, bishops, knights and castles, is like a history lesson about the Middle Ages. The pawns are the serfs − the first pieces to be sacrificed. Chess was brought to Spain by the Moors. By 1000 AD it had spread throughout Europe.

11th-century chess piece

Chess board

◄ Feudal Life

This medieval painting shows serfs in the fields, while in the background their lord's castle towers over them.

A Hard Life

In the Middle Ages, poor people had no rights. Most struggled just to stay alive. They had to work the land and were not allowed to leave their lord.

A lord's castle, often built in a high place, was a daily reminder of his power over them.

▲ The Great Charter

In a document known as the Magna Carta (1215), King John of England agreed that even a king must obey the law and give rights to his barons. Later, these rights were given to all free people.

Medieval women had few ► rights. Most marriages were about money and land, not love, and a woman's main job was to provide children. Many couples were married at fourteen.

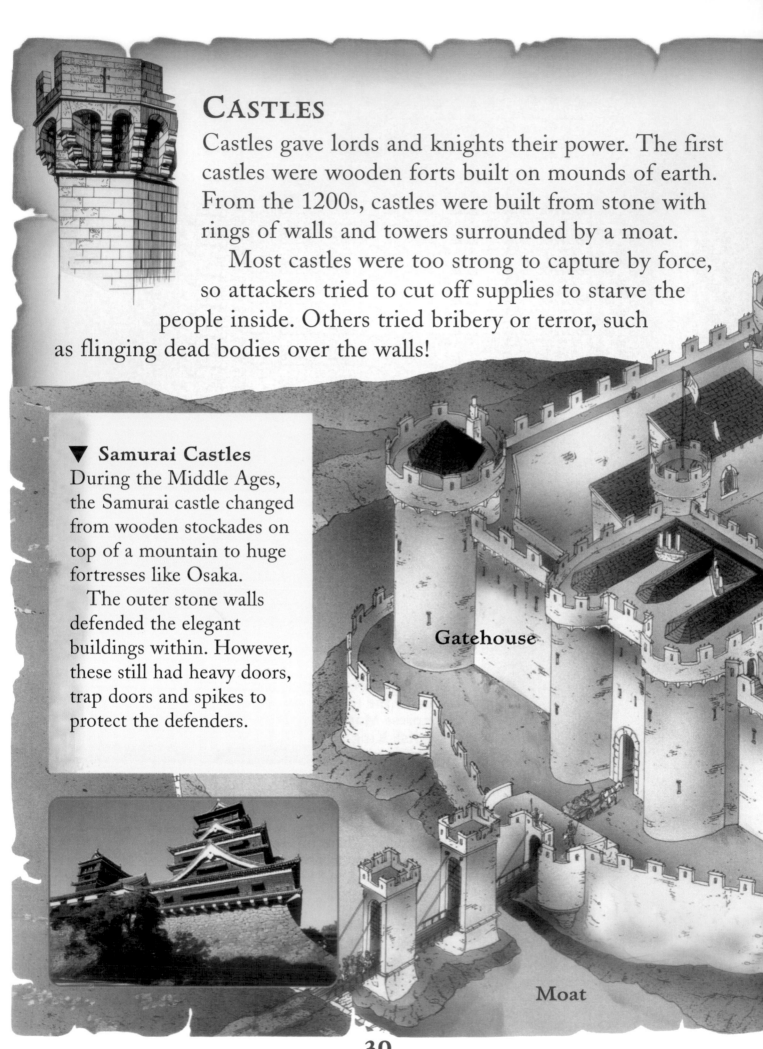

CASTLES

Castles gave lords and knights their power. The first castles were wooden forts built on mounds of earth. From the 1200s, castles were built from stone with rings of walls and towers surrounded by a moat.

Most castles were too strong to capture by force, so attackers tried to cut off supplies to starve the people inside. Others tried bribery or terror, such as flinging dead bodies over the walls!

▼ Samurai Castles

During the Middle Ages, the Samurai castle changed from wooden stockades on top of a mountain to huge fortresses like Osaka.

The outer stone walls defended the elegant buildings within. However, these still had heavy doors, trap doors and spikes to protect the defenders.

Gatehouse

Moat

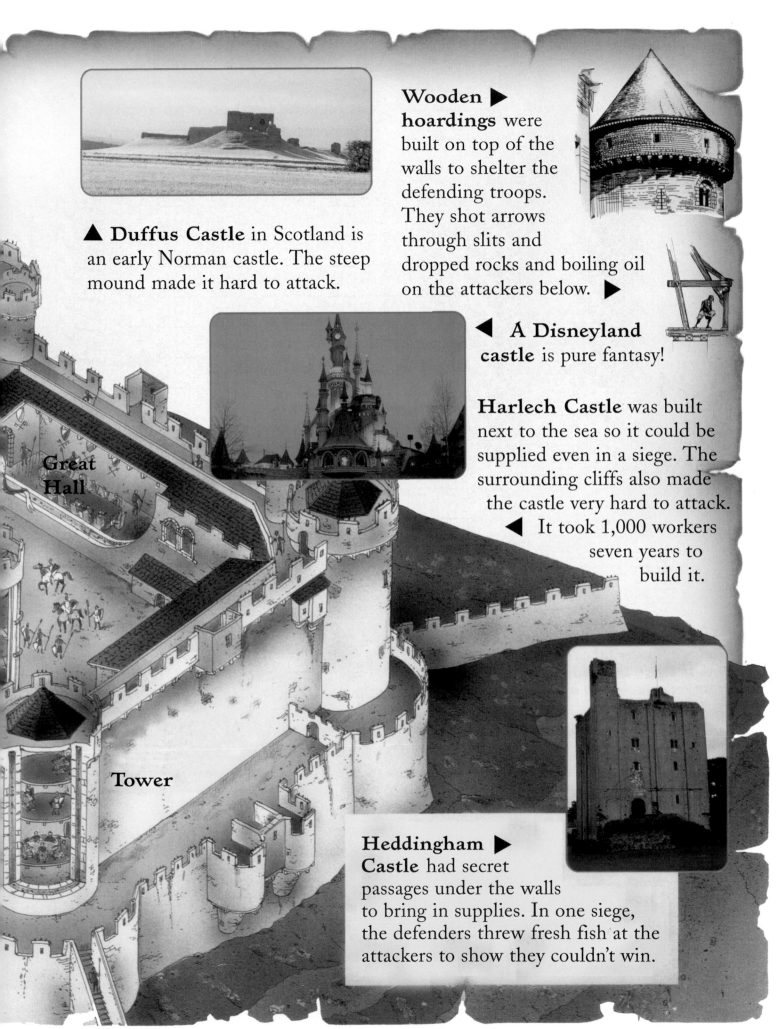

▲ Duffus Castle in Scotland is an early Norman castle. The steep mound made it hard to attack.

Wooden ▶ hoardings were built on top of the walls to shelter the defending troops. They shot arrows through slits and dropped rocks and boiling oil on the attackers below. ▶

◀ A Disneyland castle is pure fantasy!

Harlech Castle was built next to the sea so it could be supplied even in a siege. The surrounding cliffs also made the castle very hard to attack. ◀ It took 1,000 workers seven years to build it.

Great Hall

Tower

Heddingham ▶ Castle had secret passages under the walls to bring in supplies. In one siege, the defenders threw fresh fish at the attackers to show they couldn't win.

TOURNAMENTS

To help them train for battle, 40-50 knights fought mock battles in teams. There were few rules and it was every man for himself. Though stricter rules were introduced to prevent bad injuries, it was still a very dangerous sport. Nonetheless, tournaments were very popular as they gave young knights a chance to show off their fighting skills. The most popular fight was jousting, in which two knights used lances to knock each other to the ground.

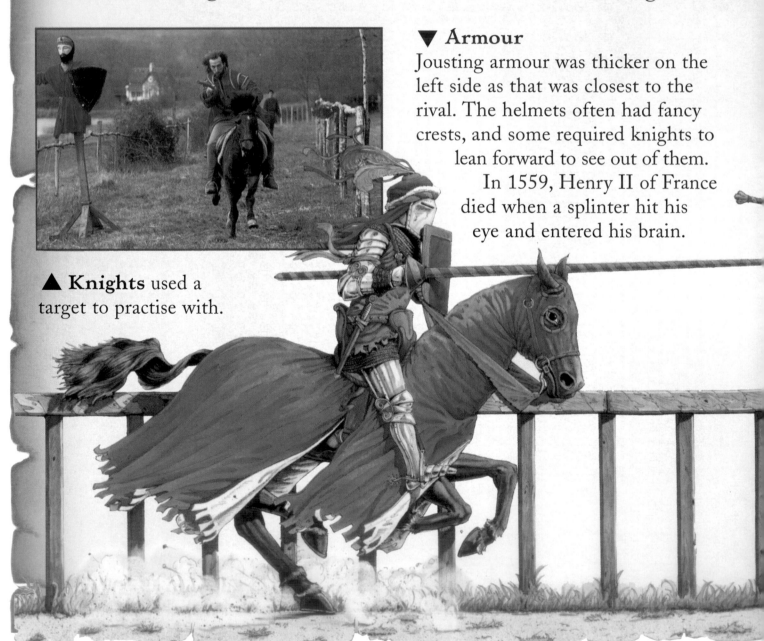

▼ Armour
Jousting armour was thicker on the left side as that was closest to the rival. The helmets often had fancy crests, and some required knights to lean forward to see out of them.

In 1559, Henry II of France died when a splinter hit his eye and entered his brain.

▲ **Knights** used a target to practise with.

▲ A war horse was a knight's key to survival, so he rode the best horse he could find. But caring for a fine war horse cost a lot of money.

▲ Jousting

From the 1420s, the two knights were separated by a low fence, the "tilt". Heralds announced the competitors, then they charged at each other with blunted lances. The winner won by knocking his opponent to the ground.

▲ A Lady's Champion

Jousting was a big event watched by ladies and a large crowd of common people. Before a tournament began, knights might take a scarf from a lady, known as a favour. They then tied this to their arm to show they were the lady's champion.

GUNPOWDER AND GUNS

The invention of gunpowder led to terrifying new weapons. By the 1400s, cannons could reduce a castle to rubble. While plate armour protected against pistols and muskets, it was expensive. Knights were gradually replaced by full-paid foot soldiers who were paid with money rather than land.

Tournaments, knighthoods and chivalry were still popular, but the age of the knight was over.

Foot soldier 1650

▼ **Giant Cannon**
The first cannons were used in China and reached Europe in the 1200s. Some cannons were huge – the Great Turkish Bombard used in 1453 at the siege of Constantinople had a crew of 200 men!

By the 1500s, cannons became lighter and could be pulled onto the battlefield.

▲ **Early cannons** often exploded unexpectedly. They were a danger to the men firing them as well as the enemy.

◀ Tudor Jousting

Jousting was a popular sport among the rich until the 1700s. When King Henry VIII met the French king Francis I in 1520, they celebrated their friendship with a tournament. Henry VIII had to retire from jousting after a bad accident in 1536.

Singing Knights ▶

Knights disappeared from the battlefield 500 years ago, but the legends of King Arthur stayed popular. His story was even made into a musical, *Camelot*!

◀ Don Quixote

By the time Miguel de Cervantes wrote his book *Don Quixote* in 1605, the age of knights was long past. The hero is an old gentleman who wants to do brave deeds like the knights of old. But too much reading and not enough sleep have clouded his mind. Joined by his neighbour, Sancho Panza, he attacks windmills after mistaking them for giants!

Arise, Sir Knight!

From around 1560, the word knight was used as  an honour rather than to describe mounted warriors. ▶

PART 4: ALL CHANGE – CAVALRY

By the 1600s, knights no longer ruled in battle, but heavy cavalry could still deliver a knockout blow once the enemy line was broken. Troops on light, fast horses were also used for scouting and chasing fleeing enemies. Mounted troops known as dragoons fought with pistols and muskets.

Cavalrymen came from rich families as it was still expensive to own a horse, but they had to follow orders like everyone else.

Dragoons

Dragoons ▶ fought from a horse and on foot. Their name came from the *dragon* musket, which "breathed fire" when shot. Dragoons were often used against rioters or smugglers as mobile foot soldiers.
.

Sabre

◀ Pistols or Swords?
In the 1540s, cavalry rode up to the enemy, shot at them with pistols, then rode away to reload. However, this tactic, known as the *caracole*, never worked as well as a cavalry charge with swords or lances.

Musket

Polish Hussars were the most feared cavalry in Europe for 200 years. They had wings attached to their saddles that made a terrifying noise as they charged.

◀ The Lion of the North

In the 1600s, Swedish king Gustav II Adolph led his armies for 20 years. Known as the "Lion of the North", he organised his army so that infantry (foot soldiers), cavalry and artillery (cannons) all worked closely together.

He died in 1632, leading a cavalry charge that got lost in a smog of mist and gunpowder smoke.

Battle of Waterloo

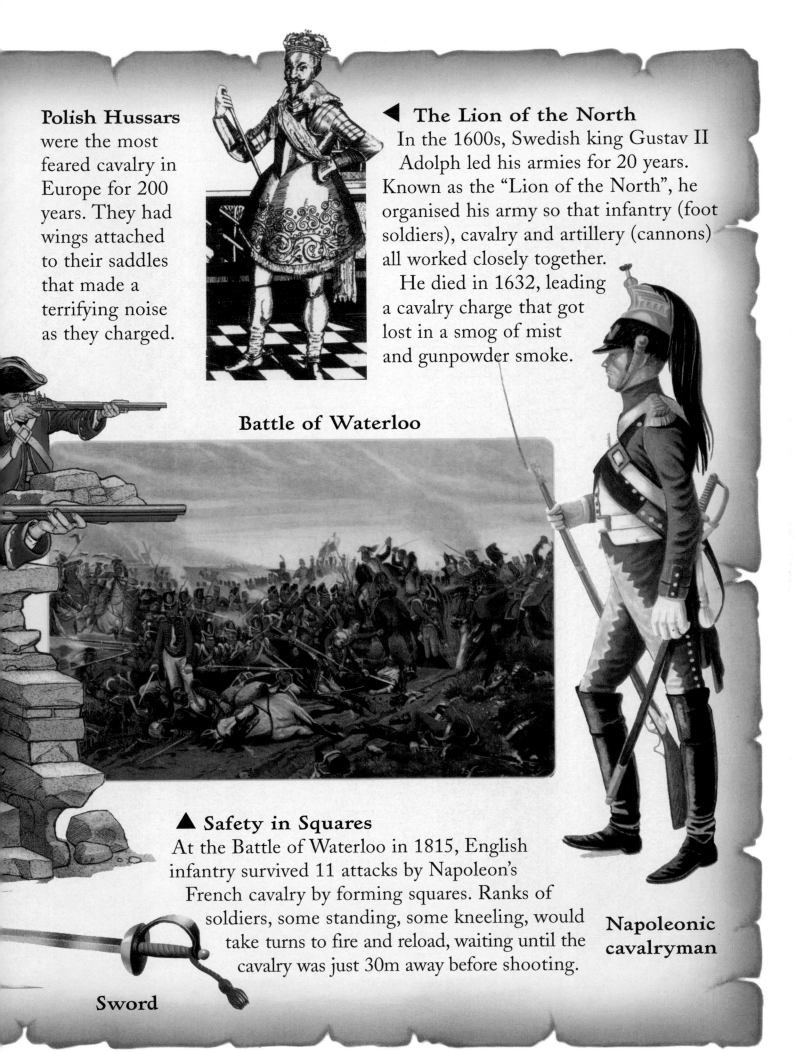

▲ Safety in Squares

At the Battle of Waterloo in 1815, English infantry survived 11 attacks by Napoleon's French cavalry by forming squares. Ranks of soldiers, some standing, some kneeling, would take turns to fire and reload, waiting until the cavalry was just 30m away before shooting.

Napoleonic cavalryman

Sword

THE KNIGHTS OF AMERICA

Horses were a key weapon for the Spanish conquistadors (conquerors) who captured the Aztec and Inca Empires in the 1600s.

When the Spanish landed, there were no horses in America. To the local peoples, their horsemen seemed half-man, half-god. With less than 600 men and just 15 horses, Hernán Cortés captured an Aztec Empire of 5 million people in 1521.

▲ **Jaguar and Eagle** warriors were Aztec knights who fought on foot. They wore leather armour and fought with stone weapons.

Hernán Cortés

▼ **Aztec weapons** were designed to knock out their enemies, not kill them, as the Aztecs wanted prisoners to sacrifice to their gods.

Francisco Pizarro

▲ **Conquering Peru**
In 1532, conquistador Francisco Pizarro captured the vast Inca Empire in Peru with 63 horsemen and 200 foot soldiers. Before battle, his captain, Hernando De Soto, performed stunts on his horse to terrify the Inca generals.

Aztec club

▼ **Native American Warriors**
Just 150 years after Cortés landed, millions of wild horses roamed the Great Plains. Native American tribes, such as the Comanche and Cheyenne, quickly learned to use horses and became skilled riders.

A warrior's rank was shown by the markings on his horse and clothes and the number of eagle feathers on his war bonnet.

Comanche warrior

Shawnee club

Iroquois club

Knife

Bow and arrows

Tomahawk

A short bow was the main weapon used by Native American warriors, along with clubs, tomahawks and knives.

Night Rider ▶
Horses have played a big role in American history. In 1775, Paul Revere rode all night to warn American patriots that British soldiers were about to attack the town of Lexington, Massachusetts.

THE COSSACKS

Light cavalry was used in battle until the 1900s, despite the invention of deadly new weapons such as the machine gun.

Russia used Cossacks to defend its borders and put down rebellions. The Cossacks were related to the tribes that swept across Asia in the Middle Ages. These skilled horsemen fought with sabres called *shashka*, lances and bows and arrows.

◀ **The Caged Rebel**
The Cossacks were proud of their freedom. In 1773, they rebelled, led by Yemelyan Pugachev, who pretended to be Tsar Peter III. After he was defeated in 1775, Pugachev was taken to Moscow in a metal cage, then executed.

▼ **Cossack dances** appear in many Russian ballets.

Cossack

Bengal Lancers

In India, the British used light cavalry to guard the northwest frontier against a possible attack by Russia. As well their famous lances, the Bengal Lancers fought with swords and short rifles known as carbines.

Polo mallet and ball

A Sport for the Rich

The sport of polo is like hockey on horseback. It was first played by Persian cavalrymen around 500 BC. With up to 100 players, it was like a small battle! Later, the sport was played by rich nobles who could afford horses.

In the 1850s, British cavalry officers in India took up the game and spread it around the world.

Polo match

Bullfighting ▶

Horses are also used in bullfighting. Picadors on horseback stab the bull with lances, making it weak but angry, before the matador kills it with his sword.

Before 1909, the horses had no protection and were often gored by the bull's horns.

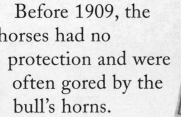

Bengal Lancer

Poster for a Bullfight

CHARGE!

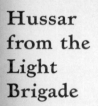

During the Battle of Balaclava in 1854, the English cavalry were told to charge the Russian cannons at the end of the valley. Though shot at from three sides, the 673 men of the Light Brigade kept going. In a few minutes, some 250 of them were killed or wounded. Though brave, the attack showed how useless cavalry had become against modern weapons.

Hussar from the Light Brigade

▼ The Boys in Blue

In the movies, the US cavalry are heroes who drive off the "Indians" and save the day.

The real US cavalrymen were known as "dog-faced soldiers". They did protect settlers and railway workers from attack but some units also carried out vicious raids.

In 1864, an attack on a peaceful Cheyenne and Arapaho village near Sand Creek, Colorado, killed 200 women, children and elderly men.

Charge of the Light Brigade ▲
When the English poet Alfred Tennyson read about Balaclava and the ride into the "Valley of Death", he wrote his famous poem, *The Charge of the Light Brigade*. His version made the attack seem heroic rather than foolish.

During the **American Civil War** (1861-1865), quick-firing rifles, cannons and machine guns meant that cavalry charges decided few battles. By now, troops could be moved quickly by train rather than on horses.

The Final Charge? ▼

Light cavalry was used in battle even in the 20th century. When World War Two started in 1939, the Polish army still had mounted soldiers. On the first day of the war, Polish lancers successfully charged German infantry, but stood no chance against armoured vehicles.

However, most armies still used horses to carry equipment and also for scouting.

Polish lancers

▼ **Today's cavalry regiments** fight in tanks rather than on horseback. The first tanks, used during World War One, were very slow. But modern tanks are fast and heavily armoured − just like the knights of old!

THE KNIGHT LIVES ON!

Though the days of the mounted warrior were finally ended by tanks and machine guns, the idea of the knight lives on. In many European countries, people are still honoured by being knighted. Books, films and games still feature knights in shining armour. Even stories set in the future, such as Star Wars, have their own Jedi "knights".

World War One "dogfight"

▼ **Cavalry skills** are still taught in some regiments.

Flying Heroes ▲
Pilots who fought in World War One were called the "Knights of the Skies" as they fought deadly one-to-one battles in the air.

The pilots respected each other as they knew the dangers of flying. Many were killed by faulty planes and a lack of parachutes rather than by enemy attacks.

Knighthood

The English Queen still honours her citizens by "knighting" them, though most have never held a sword or ridden a horse in their life!

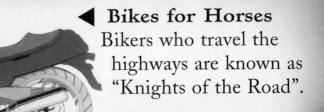

◀ ### Bikes for Horses

Bikers who travel the highways are known as "Knights of the Road".

Some **lords** still live in the castles built when their ancestors were knights in armour. ▶

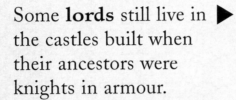

◀ ### Jedi Knights

The Jedi in the Star Wars movies fight with light sabres rather than swords and follow a strict code of honour – just like knights of old.

Jedi are expected to use the "force" for good and to defend the weak, but never for their own gain.

Police Knights ▶

Mounted officers are often used to police large crowds.

The Canadian Mounted Police, or "Mounties", are famous for "always getting their man" - a tribute to their determination and courage.

KNIGHTS GLOSSARY

Baron – A feudal lord.
Breastplate – The piece of armour covering the chest.
Bushido – A samurai's code of honour.
Chain-mail – Armour made from hundreds of linked loops of metal.
Chivalry – The knight's code of honour.
Coat of arms – A knight's family badge, worn on or over his armour.
Conquistador – A Spanish conqueror of the New World (America) in the 1500s.
Cossack – A mounted warrior from southern Russia.
Crusade – A campaign by Christian knights to recapture Jerusalem.

Dragoon – A mounted soldier armed with sword and a short musket (above).
Feudal system – A system of giving out land in return for support (in war).
Heavy cavalry – Soldiers mounted on large horses, used for cavalry charges.
Heraldry – A system of designs and badges used by knights (left).
Holy Grail – The cup which Christ was said to have used during the Last Supper.

Hussar – Light cavalry, originally from Hungary.
Infantry – Foot soldiers.
Jousting – Fighting with lances in a tournament.
Lance – Long spear carried by cavalry.
Light cavalry – Soldiers mounted on smaller, faster horses used for scouting or chasing fleeing enemies.
Lists – The field where jousting took place.
Mercenary – A soldier who fights for pay.
Mountie – A Royal Canadian Mounted Policeman.
Pike – A long pole with a metal spike at the end.

Pilgrim – Someone who travels to visit a holy shrine.
Samurai – Japanese knight (above).
Spurs – Spikes worn on a rider's heel to control a horse (below).
Squire – A knight's young servant.
Tilt – The fence between two jousting knights.
Tournament – A fighting contest held in front of a crowd.

KNIGHTS TIMELINE

12,000 BC Humans first train horses to work for them.

3000 BC Chariot (left) is invented.

776 BC Horse races part of first Olympic Games.

1st century AD Saddle is invented.

218 AD Hannibal crosses the Alps with 30,000 men and 37 elephants.

378 AD Goth heavy cavalry defeats the Romans at Adrianople.

4th century AD The stirrup is invented in China.

5th to 11th centuries Asian tribes invade Europe.

6th century King Arthur may have lived at this time.

8th–9th centuries Frankish kings develop the feudal system.

900 to 1400 Knights rule the battlefield in Europe (right).

1066 Saxon foot soldiers are beaten by Norman knights at the Battle of Hastings.

1095 Pope Urban II calls for the First Crusade.

12th century Geoffrey of Monmouth creates the legend of King Arthur.

1185 Minamoto Yoritomo becomes shogun. For the next 700 years, the Samurai dominate Japan.

13th century Genghis Khan's mongols (right) sweep across Asia.

Mid-13th century Plate armour begins to replace chain-mail.

14th century Invention of gunpowder and cannons leads to end of castles.

1415 English longbows defeat the French knights at Agincourt.

1512 French cannons destroy Spanish knights at the Battle of Ravenna.

16th century Spanish Conquistadors reintroduce the horse to America.

1600 Native Americans first learn to ride horses.

1620s Gustav II Adolph combines cavalry with infantry and artillery.

17th century First dragoons: riders armed with guns.

18th to 19th centuries Russian army uses Cossacks to protect borders (below).

1854 The Charge of the Light Brigade at the Battle of Balaclava.

1914–1918 Planes first fight in the air and tank invented during World War I.

1939 Polish lancers fight at the start of World War II.

INDEX

Photocredits (*Abbreviations: t – top, m – middle, b – bottom, r – right, l – left*).
Cover, 4-5, 7b, 10tl, 12-13, 14m, 18, 19t, 25, 26m, 28m, 29, 32t, 33, 37t & m, 39br, 40t & m, 43t & br: Mary Evans Picture Library. 6, 7t, 15, 16, 17, 21b, 31m, 32m, 36, 41, 44, 45tr & br: Frank Spooner Pictures. 8t, 21t & 28-29: Ancient Art & Architecture Collection. 8b: Paramount Pictures (courtesy Kobal Collection). 9: MGM (courtesy Kobal Collection). 11tr: 20th Century Fox (courtesy Kobal Collection). 14b & 31t & b: Stewart Ross. 19b & 27t & m: Ronald Grant Archive. 23 & 42-43: Bridgeman Art Library. 27: Columbia/Warner (courtesy Kobal Collection). 28t & bl & br: Roger Vlitos. 30: Eye Ubiquitous. 35t: Hulton Deutsch. 35m: Warner Brothers (courtesy Kobal Collection). 43bl: Tom Donovan Military Pictures. 45ml: Lucas Films/20th Century Fox (courtesy Kobal Collection).